AF323598

T H I S   J O U R N A L   B E L O N G S
T O :

www.qualifieddaughters.com

DATE 

SERMON TITLE

SCRIPTURE

NOTES

DATE

SERMON TITLE

SCRIPTURE

NOTES

DATE

SERMON TITLE

SCRIPTURE

NOTES

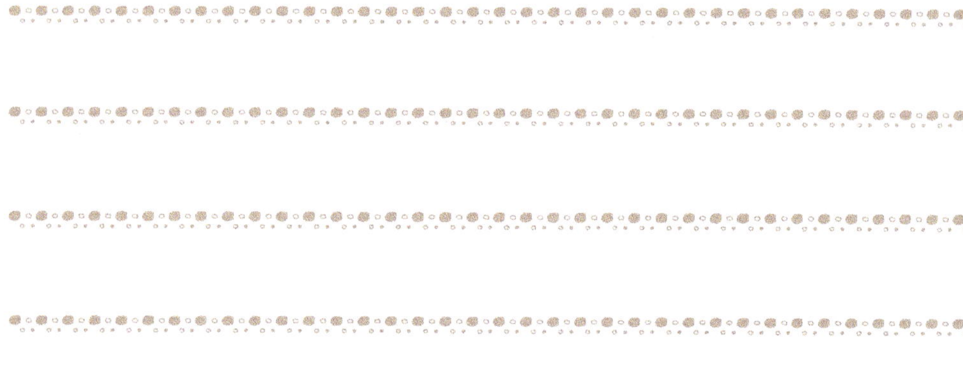

DATE 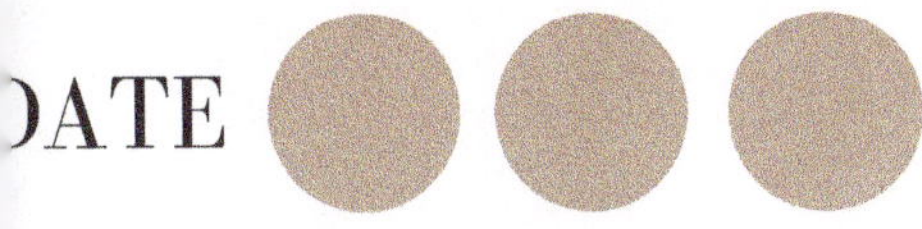

SERMON TITLE

SCRIPTURE

NOTES

SERMON TITLE

SCRIPTURE

NOTES

DATE

SERMON TITLE

SCRIPTURE

NOTES

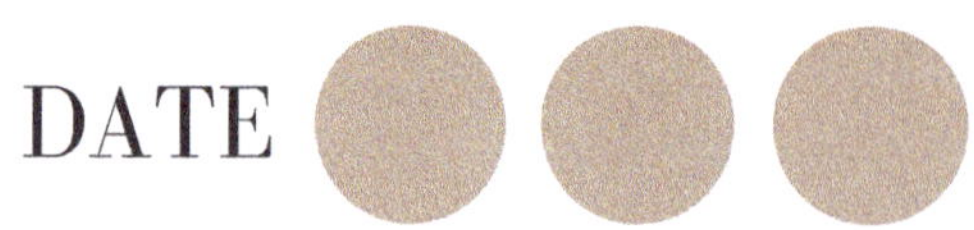

DATE

SERMON TITLE

SCRIPTURE

NOTES

DATE 

SERMON TITLE

SCRIPTURE

NOTES

DATE

SERMON TITLE

SCRIPTURE

NOTES

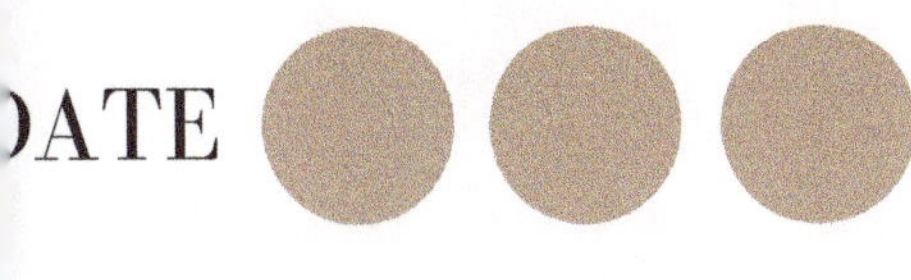

DATE

SERMON TITLE

SCRIPTURE

NOTES

DATE

SERMON TITLE

SCRIPTURE

NOTES

DATE 

SERMON TITLE

SCRIPTURE

NOTES

SERMON TITLE

SCRIPTURE

NOTES

DATE

SERMON TITLE

SCRIPTURE

NOTES

DATE

SERMON TITLE

SCRIPTURE

NOTES

DATE 

SERMON TITLE

SCRIPTURE

NOTES

DATE 

SERMON TITLE

SCRIPTURE

NOTES

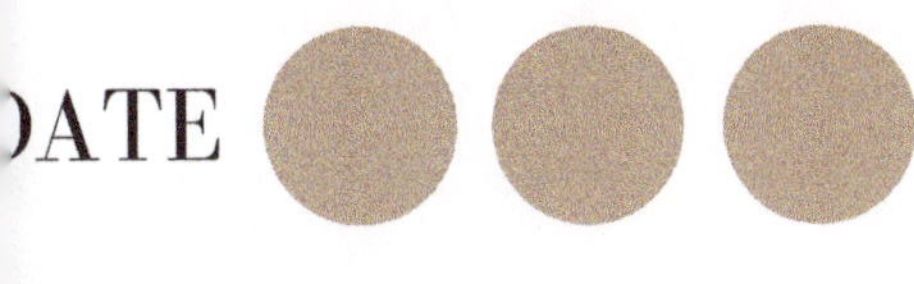

DATE

SERMON TITLE

SCRIPTURE

NOTES

DATE

SERMON TITLE

SCRIPTURE

NOTES

DATE 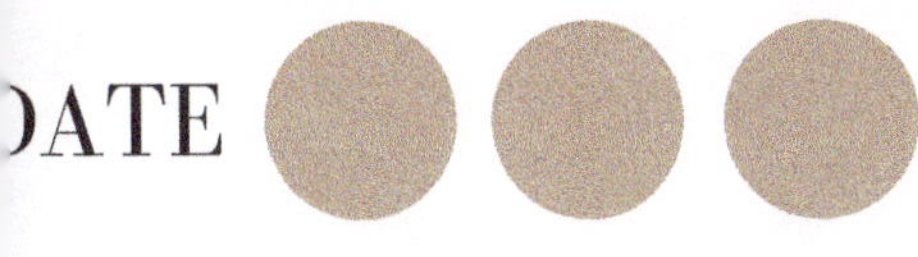

SERMON TITLE

SCRIPTURE

NOTES

DATE

SERMON TITLE

SCRIPTURE

NOTES

DATE

SERMON TITLE

SCRIPTURE

NOTES

DATE

SERMON TITLE

SCRIPTURE

NOTES

DATE 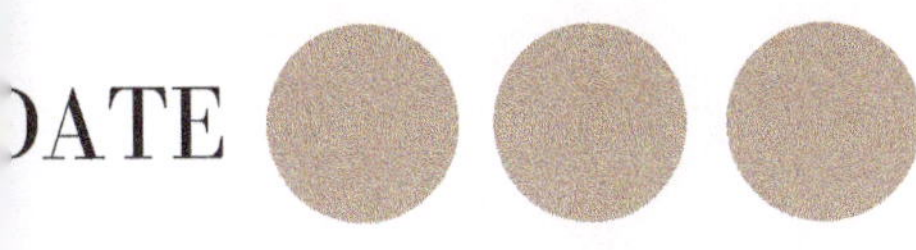

SERMON TITLE

SCRIPTURE

NOTES

DATE

SERMON TITLE

SCRIPTURE

NOTES

DATE 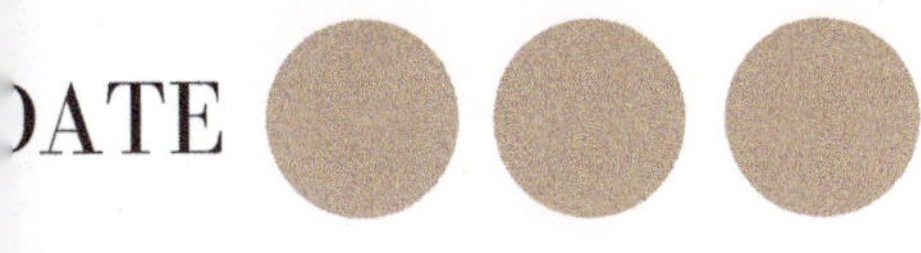

SERMON TITLE

SCRIPTURE

NOTES

DATE

SERMON TITLE

SCRIPTURE

NOTES

DATE 

SERMON TITLE

SCRIPTURE

NOTES

DATE

SERMON TITLE

SCRIPTURE

NOTES

DATE

SERMON TITLE

SCRIPTURE

NOTES

DATE

SERMON TITLE

SCRIPTURE

NOTES

DATE 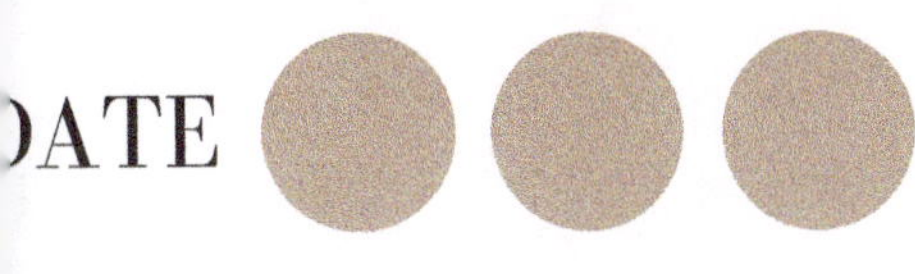

SERMON TITLE

SCRIPTURE

NOTES

DATE

SERMON TITLE

SCRIPTURE

NOTES

DATE 

SERMON TITLE

SCRIPTURE

NOTES

DATE 

SERMON TITLE

SCRIPTURE

NOTES

DATE

SERMON TITLE

SCRIPTURE

NOTES

DATE

SERMON TITLE

SCRIPTURE

NOTES

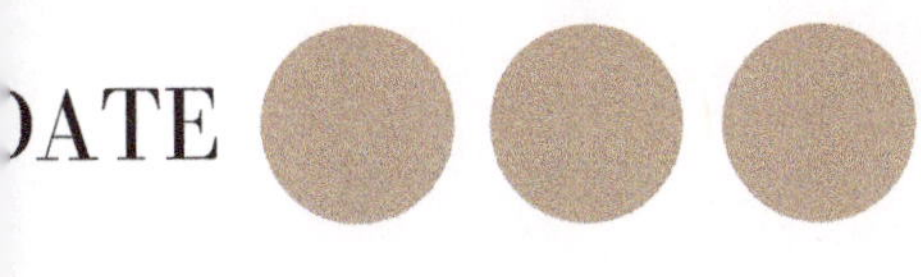

DATE

SERMON TITLE

SCRIPTURE

NOTES

DATE 

SERMON TITLE

SCRIPTURE

NOTES

DATE 

SERMON TITLE

SCRIPTURE

NOTES

DATE 

SERMON TITLE

SCRIPTURE

NOTES

DATE

SERMON TITLE

SCRIPTURE

NOTES

DATE

SERMON TITLE

SCRIPTURE

NOTES

DATE

SERMON TITLE

SCRIPTURE

NOTES

DATE 

SERMON TITLE

SCRIPTURE

NOTES

DATE 

SERMON TITLE

SCRIPTURE

NOTES

DATE

SERMON TITLE

SCRIPTURE

NOTES

DATE 

SERMON TITLE

SCRIPTURE

NOTES

DATE

SERMON TITLE

SCRIPTURE

NOTES

DATE 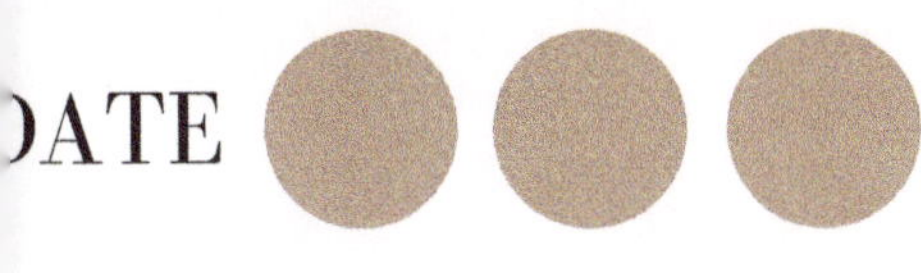

SERMON TITLE

SCRIPTURE

NOTES

SERMON TITLE

SCRIPTURE

NOTES

DATE 

SERMON TITLE

SCRIPTURE

NOTES

SERMON TITLE

SCRIPTURE

NOTES

DATE 

SERMON TITLE

SCRIPTURE

NOTES

SERMON TITLE

SCRIPTURE

NOTES

DATE 

SERMON TITLE

SCRIPTURE

NOTES

DATE 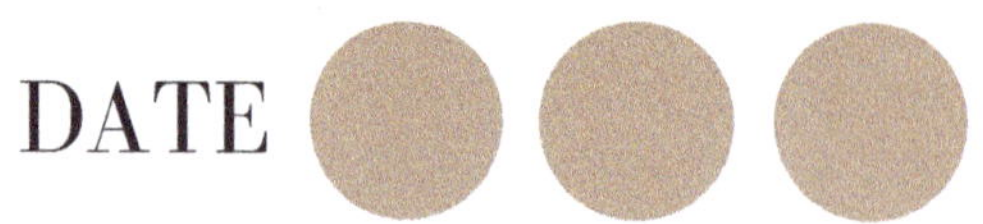

SERMON TITLE

SCRIPTURE

NOTES

DATE 

SERMON TITLE

SCRIPTURE

NOTES

DATE

SERMON TITLE

SCRIPTURE

NOTES

DATE

SERMON TITLE

SCRIPTURE

NOTES

DATE

SERMON TITLE

SCRIPTURE

NOTES

DATE 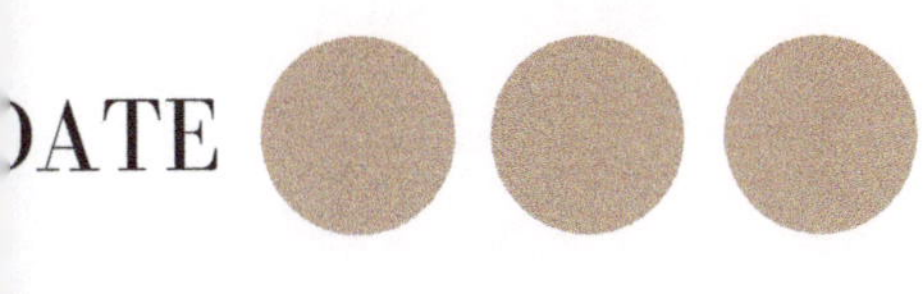

SERMON TITLE

SCRIPTURE

NOTES

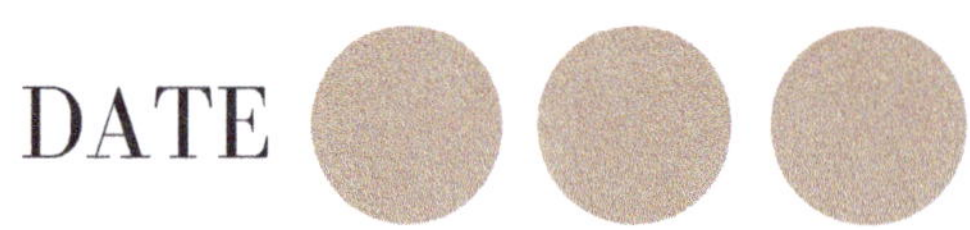

DATE

SERMON TITLE

SCRIPTURE

NOTES

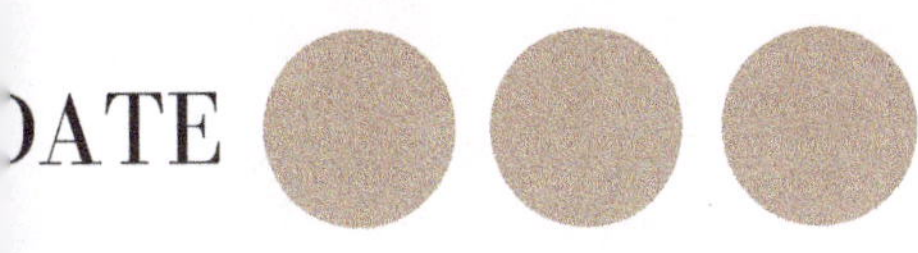

DATE

SERMON TITLE

SCRIPTURE

NOTES

SERMON TITLE

SCRIPTURE

NOTES

DATE 

SERMON TITLE

SCRIPTURE

NOTES

DATE 

SERMON TITLE

SCRIPTURE

NOTES

DATE

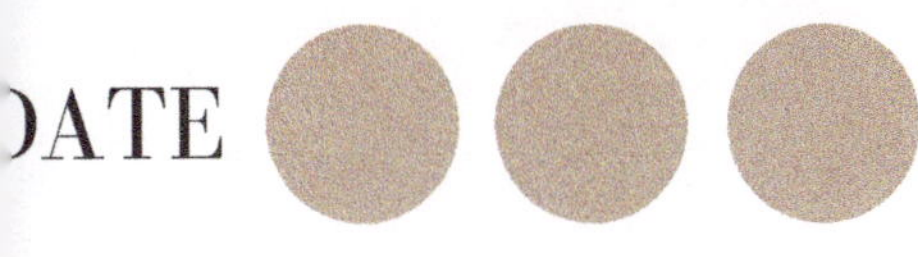

SERMON TITLE

SCRIPTURE

NOTES

DATE

SERMON TITLE

SCRIPTURE

NOTES

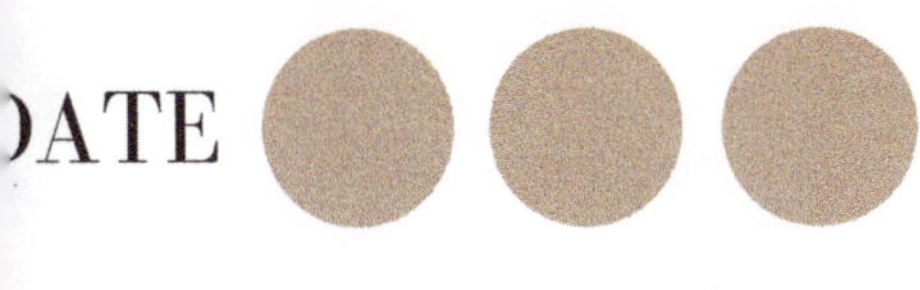

DATE

SERMON TITLE

SCRIPTURE

NOTES

DATE

SERMON TITLE

SCRIPTURE

NOTES

DATE

SERMON TITLE

SCRIPTURE

NOTES

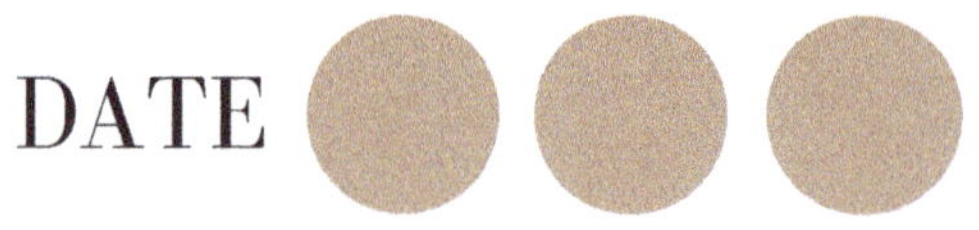

DATE

SERMON TITLE

SCRIPTURE

NOTES

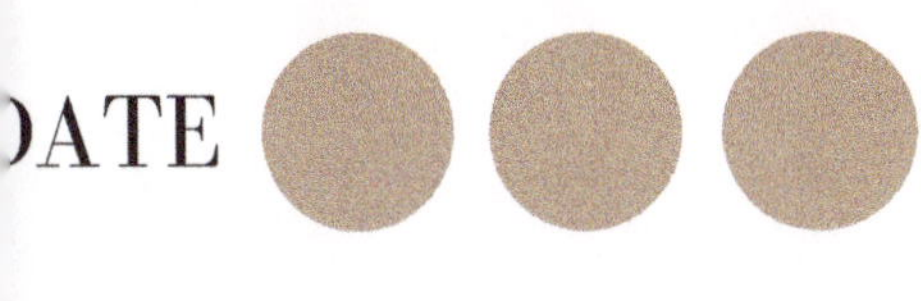

DATE

SERMON TITLE

SCRIPTURE

NOTES

DATE 

SERMON TITLE

SCRIPTURE

NOTES

DATE 

SERMON TITLE

SCRIPTURE

NOTES

DATE 

SERMON TITLE

SCRIPTURE

NOTES

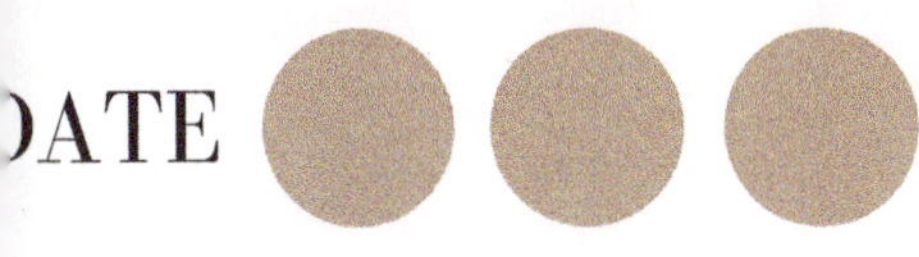

DATE

SERMON TITLE

SCRIPTURE

NOTES

SERMON TITLE

DATE

SERMON TITLE

SCRIPTURE

NOTES

SERMON TITLE

SCRIPTURE

NOTES

SERMON TITLE

SCRIPTURE

NOTES

DATE 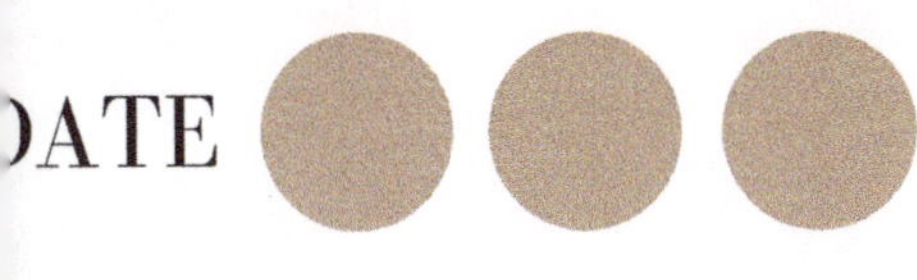

SERMON TITLE

SCRIPTURE

NOTES

DATE

SERMON TITLE

SCRIPTURE

NOTES

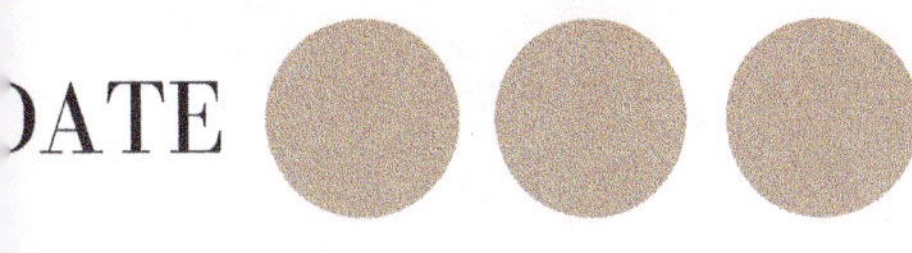

DATE

SERMON TITLE

SCRIPTURE

NOTES

DATE 

SERMON TITLE

SCRIPTURE

NOTES

DATE 

SERMON TITLE

SCRIPTURE

NOTES

SERMON TITLE

SCRIPTURE

NOTES

DATE 

SERMON TITLE

SCRIPTURE

NOTES

CPSIA information can be obtained
at www.ICGtesting.com
Printed in the USA
BVHW021834301120
594481BV00011B/300

9 781735 934327